QUARTER HORSES

Dorothy Hinshaw Patent

photographs by William Muñoz *and others*

HOLIDAY HOUSE/NEW YORK

To JOEL *and* LYNN GLEASON

ACKNOWLEDGMENTS

The author and photographer would like to thank the following people, who were kind enough to let them use photos of them and/or their animals: Joel and Lynn Gleason (frontis, pg. 41); Bernard Hakes (pp. 4, 24, 25, 26); Mary Moranville (pp. 9, 35); Sunland Park, NM (pp. 10, 71, 72, 73, 74, 75, 76, 78; Ray and Wendy Norgaard (pg. 17); Sandy Muñoz (pg. 26); Carl Moss (pp. 29, 32); Keith Cable (pp. 21, 30); Cindy and Buddy Westphal and family (pp. 31, 53, 55, 56, 57, 58, 59, 60, 61, 64, 65); Gilbert Holyoak (pp. 33, 37, 68); Montana High School Rodeo (pp. 7, 44, 45, 46, 47, 48); Pam and Marvin Walchuck (pp. 49, 50, 51); John Nash (pp. 62, 66); Bay Meadows, CA (pp. 69, 70); and Hal Fullerton (pg. 79).

We would also like to thank Barbara Baker, Joel Gleason, and Buddy Westphal for reading and commenting on parts of the manuscript.

Library of Congress Cataloging in Publication Data

Patent, Dorothy Hinshaw
    Quarter horses.

    Includes index.
    Summary: An introduction to the quarter horse, the most popular breed of horse in the world.
    1. Quarter horse—Juvenile literature. [1. Quarter horse. 2. Horses] I. Muñoz, William, ill. II. Title.
SF293.Q3P38 1985   636.1'33   85-904
ISBN 0-8234-0573-7

Contents

QUARTER HORSES

1

The All-Around Horse

The American Quarter Horse is the most popular breed of horse in the world, and with good reason. The Quarter Horse is strong, sure-footed, and even-tempered. It is a superb animal athlete and can stop and turn in an instant or run at breakneck speed for a quarter mile. Quarter Horses are prized for their natural talent in working cattle and for their gentle disposition as family pleasure horses. They are also valued highly for their speed on the racetrack, with one of the highest stakes in horse racing—$1,000,000—going every Labor Day to the winner of the famous All American Futurity at Ruidoso Downs, New Mexico.

While the American Quarter Horse has been around for a long time, it did not become an official breed until 1940, when its own association was founded for keeping records on

This Quarter Horse foal, running with its mother,
could grow up to be a cow horse, a family horse,
a show horse, or even a racer.

the breeding and accomplishments of these versatile horses. Since then, more than two million animals have been officially registered as American Quarter Horses. This number does not include horses that are mostly of Quarter Horse ancestry or those whose owners did not take the trouble and go to the expense of having their animals officially registered. Quarter Horses are popular in countries other than the United States, especially ones like Australia, where large herds of cattle are raised.

Quarter Horse Beginnings

The American Quarter Horse is clearly a product of the United States, one whose history is closely tied to the settlement and expansion of this country. Like so many American accomplishments, this special breed is the result of the mixture of influences from different countries that went into the making of America. Even before the establishment of the Virginia Colony by the English, horses were important on this continent to the Spanish and the Indians. By 1671, there were already close to 10,000 horses in Virginia, and among these were the first Quarter Horses, already known and respected for their speed.

Competition has always been a part of human society, and many people have found horse racing one of the most exciting and satisfying kinds of competition.

In the colonies, a new type of race was developed that suited the limitations of colonial life and the talents of colonial horses. A short race covering only a quarter of a mile, run straight along a road such as the main street of a town, became the standard contest for judging a horse's speed. Roads were few and poorly built, and the colonists could not spend the time and money necessary to build special tracks at which races could be held. The quarter-mile stretch was a practical length. Besides, quick bursts of speed were more important in horses used for practical purposes such as herding cattle than was the ability to keep up speed over long distances.

The goal of those developing the Quarter Horse has always been the same—to produce a reliable working animal

Eclipse and Shakespeare, two colonial horses, prepare for a match race. COURTESY OF THE KEENELAND LIBRARY

that could put on rapid bursts of speed. The result is a solidly built but not tall horse, with strong, muscular legs, shoulders, and rump. The Quarter Horse carries its head low, which helps it keep its balance and footing on the rough terrain where it so often has to work. Quarter Horses are heavier for their height than any other breed of saddle horse, an indication of how much hard-working muscle their bodies carry.

Descriptions of the early colonial horses sound very much like that of the modern Quarter Horse. When the Quarter Horse was officially established in 1940, Robert Denhardt and Helen Michaelis made a thorough study of breed origins and came to the conclusion that the traits of the Quarter Horse were already recognizable by about 1665.

The strong muscles of the Quarter Horse
are clearly shown on this animal.

Changes and improvements, however, have been occurring throughout the history of the breed. The first horses brought to the English colonies were of various breeds. Galloways, sturdy horses from the British Isles, were popular as were horses called Hobbies. Spanish horses captured from French colonies were also involved in the early mixture. During the 1700s, ponies raised by the Cherokee and Chickasaw Indians were bred with the colonial horses. These Indians lived between the northern British colonies and the Spanish settlers in Florida, to the south. Their strong, sturdy ponies were derived mainly from Spanish stock.

Early Racing

In the 1700s, horse racing in the southern colonies, from Maryland to South Carolina, meant quarter racing. The initials C.A.Q.R.H. stood for Celebrated American Quarter Running Horse, a racer of distinction. If the last letter was an "M" instead of an "H", the animal was a mare (female horse), not a male. With little entertainment for the public enjoyment, the colonies were enthusiastic about horse racing. But American racing bore little resemblance to that in the old country. In England, racing was done by horses bred for the track. They ran exhausting contests over four-mile distances. A race often consisted of separate races, called heats, and the winner had to come in first in two out of three heats. After such races, the horses would have been too tired to perform any useful work even if it had been asked of them. Only the wealthy could afford to raise horses used exclusively for racing, and in the early days of America, few were rich. In addi-

Cedar Brook, shown here with her fine foal,
is an old-fashioned Quarter Horse, with short,
strong legs and a powerful body.

Today, Quarter Horses race on well-kept tracks instead of dirt roads.

tion, racetracks were expensive to build and maintain, and the American colonists could not afford that luxury.

In the colonies, horses were kept for practical reasons. They were primarily "using" animals, taken out to bring in the cows for milking, hitched to the buggy for a ride into town, or ridden by children many miles to school. To be worth its keep, a horse had to be able to do whatever was asked of it in terms of work. But if it was also fast, so much the better, for then the owner had a chance to make a few dollars from bets on races. All it took to set up a race was a short, straight length of road, about a quarter-mile long, and two people with fast horses.

These early Quarter Horse contests were match races run between just two horses. There were no starting gates, so the animals either began from a standing start or a running start across a starting line. The starting and finish lines were merely marks made in the dirt by dragging a stick across the road. To start the race, one rider asked the other if he was ready. If the answer was yes, the race was on, and within twenty-five seconds it was over. The horses ran their fastest for the short race, but both were still able to do whatever work was required of them during the rest of the day.

The Revolutionary War

During the Revolutionary War, many Quarter Horses served the colonists in their battles with the British, and many animals died. Since horses were vital to an army, carrying men and supplies and pulling artillery, they were killed by both armies in an effort to weaken the other side. In addition to eliminating many horses, the war interrupted both the breeding and racing of Quarter Horses. Horses that had been taken by the British and then reclaimed by the Americans were often of uncertain ancestry. As a result, the family history of many important early Quarter Horses is not completely known. This is unfortunate, for people who raise horses want to keep track of the ancestry, or bloodlines, of their animals. They want to be able to trace the bloodlines back both through the sire, or father, and the dam, or mother.

While a great many of the horses in the Northeast were killed during the war, those in the Roanoke Valley of Virginia were spared. Racing as well as careful breeding continued during the conflict, and after the war, the Roanoke Valley became an important center for Quarter Horses. Other valleys west of the Appalachian Mountains, safe from the fighting, also became important centers for breeding Quarter Horses.

By the early 1700s, quarter racing had been taken to established tracks, in addition to country roads, with regularly scheduled races. As the colonies became wealthier and more settled, horse racing became a specialized sport, with horses bred mainly for racing and earning their keep by winning races. At first, "short horse" racing—contests held over a quarter mile or less—was very popular. But with the increasing prosperity of America, distance racing also began to take hold in the more settled parts of the colonies. Expensive racing stallions, many of which would later be called founders of the American Thoroughbred horse, were imported. These horses were bred to American mares and to imported mares to produce race horses.

Janus

One of the most interesting of these stallions was Janus. Although he was a Thoroughbred, Janus looked more like a Quarter Horse. He was shorter than most distance horses and had a powerful build. Janus was born in England in 1746 and imported to Virginia about 1752. He had raced very suc-

This drawing of Janus, by Bill Moomey, is based on descriptions of the great horse by those who saw him. COURTESY OF BILL MOOMEY

cessfully but had been injured before he was brought across the Atlantic. In Virginia, he recovered his health and competed successfully in the long heat races. When he was retired from the track, Janus was first bred to long-legged, distance-racing mares, resulting in horses with the stamina to run long races. His most promising offspring, however, were mares, which were not considered as valuable as stallions, so his worth was not thought to be that much at the time. Then Quarter Horse breeders got a hold of him, and a surprising thing happened. When bred to the native short horses, especially those with Chickasaw breeding, he produced offspring with the blinding early speed necessary to win quarter races, and Janus was in great demand.

One famous Janus offspring was Twigg, a stallion Janus fathered in 1778 at the advanced age of thirty-two. Twigg was only beaten twice, and both times he carried twenty pounds more than his rival. He won considerable riches for his owner, since betting on quarter races at that time involved very large wagers, often in tobacco rather than cash. The stakes in Twigg's most challenging races ranged from 30,000 to 100,000 pounds of tobacco.

Janus's name comes from a Roman god with two different faces. The name could not have been more appropriate, for this great horse was an important founder of the two great American racing horses, the American Thoroughbred and, to a much greater degree, the American Quarter Horse.

Other stallions imported from England influenced the development of the Quarter Horse, but it was often a couple of generations later that their effects on the breed became apparent. The great sire of many outstanding distance horses,

Diomed, fathered a handsome stallion named Sir Archy (1805-1833), himself a very successful racehorse. Sir Archy's own offspring were distance horses, too, but strangely enough, his grandsons and granddaughters were very important in improving the Quarter Horse breed.

Diomed, shown here in an old drawing, was a great sire of Thoroughbreds that also was important in the development of the Quarter Horse.
REPRODUCED BY KIND PERMISSION OF
THE STEWARDS OF THE JOCKEY CLUB

2

The Quarter Horse Moves West

As the American frontier moved further and further west, the versatile, strong Quarter Horse went with it. Quarter Horses lost their importance in the East as the people there became wealthier, less dependant on horses, and more interested in distance racing. But the Quarter Horse was vital to the pioneers, and even in barely settled areas, a quarter-mile track could be found for a horse race.

While Quarter Horses continued to work and race as the frontier expanded, it was not until the mid-1800s, in Texas, that the next really important events in the development of the breed occurred. Texas was a vast land, ideal for raising large numbers of tough, independent longhorn cattle. Cattle that had escaped from Mexican ranches thrived in the wide open spaces of Texas, and the men who gathered and branded them were able to become ranchers with minimal financial investment.

Good horses were needed to work the cattle, however. The wild mustangs, descended from escaped horses, tended to be too small to work the powerful longhorns. Quarter Horses were brought in from the East to use with the cattle and to improve the local horses.

In the West today, many ranchers still use Quarter Horses to herd their cattle.

Copperbottom

The first famous Texas Quarter Horse sire was Copperbottom. Born in Pennsylvania in 1828, he was a son of Sir Archy and could be traced to Janus on his dam's side. He was a successful short-distance racer. When he was eleven years old, Copperbottom was bought by General Sam Houston, governer of what was then the independent Lone Star Republic of Texas. The horse was raced and bred by the Houston family until he died in 1860.

Shiloh

Shiloh was born in Tennessee in 1844 and brought to Texas at the age of five. He was a descendant of Sir Archy and, like him, his greatest influence was through the daughters and granddaughters he produced. Shiloh himself, however, was a very fast short horse and won many match races with fine runners. He was also bred extensively. Unfortunately, his owner did not keep good records, so the names of the mares bred to him are mostly unknown. Many famous Quarter Horses, however, are descendants of Shiloh. He lived to be thirty years old and he was apparently still strong and energetic at that age, since he died from injuries suffered in a fight with another stallion.

Steel Dust

Shiloh and Steel Dust were the two fastest sprinters in Texas during the mid-1800s. Steel Dust was born about 1844 in Kentucky and was brought to Texas as a young horse. His parentage is uncertain, but his sire is thought to trace back to Janus. Steel Dust rapidly became known as a fast horse. His reputation was sealed, however, in a famous race against a Thoroughbred born in Kentucky named Monmouth. The race was a big event, and people came from miles around, filling every bed in the small town of McKinney, where Monmouth lived. Monmouth was favored but Steel Dust won the race, proving that a Quarter Horse of unknown

King, shown here, lived from 1936 to 1958. He exhibited the powerful build of the old-style Quarter Horse. He fathered over 600 horses that became champions in all areas of Quarter Horse competition, including racing, cutting, roping, and pleasure. COURTESY AMERICAN QUARTER HORSE ASSOCIATION

breeding could run faster over a quarter mile than an expensive Kentucky Thoroughbred.

The win over Monmouth brought fame to Steel Dust, and soon a match race with Shiloh was arranged. Everybody wanted to know which of the two great horses was faster. The race was scheduled at a track near Dallas in 1855. The track had lanes and starting chutes. While the horses were in the chutes, waiting for the race to start, Steel Dust got excited and reared up. He broke a board, driving a splinter into his shoulder muscle. The race was called off, and Steel Dust never raced again. Fortunately, however, he was bred to many fine mares and left his mark on the Quarter Horse breed. Steel Dust horses had very large jaws, which they apparently inherited from the great horse himself.

The Texas Cattle Drives

During the mid-1800s, while Quarter Horses were becoming the cattle horses of Texas, railroads were being built across the American plains. In the settled Northeast, there was a shortage of beef, but in Texas, cattle abounded. Cattle in Texas were only worth two to five dollars a head. If sold in Kansas, however, the same animals were worth twenty to forty dollars each. The new railroad provided a way of getting the meat to where it was in demand, if only the cattle could be brought to the railroad. This was the beginning of the cattle drives, made famous by classic "western" films such as *Red River*. The huge King Ranch in Texas, which

In the early days of cattle ranching, the plains were open and cattle crossed miles of roadless land. Today, cattle are often herded along roads from one pasture to another, or to market.

has been important in the development of the Quarter Horse, sent millions of cattle northward starting in 1866, and other Texas ranchers did the same. The herds were often huge, with thousands of head of cattle accompanied by dozens of cowboys to control them. Quality horses were needed to herd the cattle, for the Texas Longhorn was a half-wild, skittish animal. A cowboy needed a strong, quick mount that was a match for the cattle, for his life often depended on his horse. This need for good horses encouraged the breeding of the best horses possible for the job.

As the cattle were herded northward across the plains, people could not help but notice the fine horses used by the Texas cowboys. The cattle drives helped spread knowledge about the Quarter Horse northward and westward, for these stocky, muscular horses stood out. The Steel Dust horses especially, with their distinctive powerful jaws, were easy to spot. Thus, as cattle ranches were established farther and farther west, Quarter Horses went along, and the breed became a fixture on the American frontier.

Miss Jim, 45, who won a total of 175 Grand Championships in Quarter Horse shows in the late 1960s and early 1970s, exhibits the powerful, bunched muscles favored in Quarter Horses before crossing with Thoroughbreds became popular.
COURTESY OF MICHAEL MULBERGER

3
The Life of the Quarter Horse

Quarter Horses live in many different places. Some are back-yard horses, with only a small pasture to roam in. Others are pampered show horses that spend most of their time in warm stalls. But since the Quarter Horse typically lives on a western ranch, we will take a look at the life of working Quarter Horses.

A young foal gets nourishment from it's mother's milk.

Baby horses, called foals, are born in the springtime. While race horses are often born early in the year, working horses are generally born later, when the weather has warmed up and the grass is growing. That way, the rancher does not have to worry about cold weather endangering his foals, and the mother horses will have plenty to eat. The mares and foals are left to romp, play, and graze in the pasture on their

Foals and their mothers on ranches are free to run in big pastures.

own. Unlike many horses, such as Thoroughbreds, which are handled from the time they are very young, ranch Quarter Horse foals may be touched rarely by humans for the first few months of their lives.

The working horses may be left to graze in a pasture for days between jobs, while sometimes they may have to work hard for many days in a row. Many Quarter Horses never see the inside of a barn. They live in a pasture between jobs and are let back into the pasture after working.

Even during the cold western winters, ranch horses live outside. They grow thick shaggy coats that protect them from the cold, and ranchers bring hay to them every day so they have enough to eat.

Working on the Ranch

The American Quarter Horse as it exists today was perfected as a cow horse. No other breed possesses the special combination of traits—sure-footedness, strength, agility, and calm temperament—that make the Quarter Horse ideally suited to ranch work. It can dash fast enough from a standing start to run down a wayward cow, and it is strong and heavy enough to pull against the weight of a roped calf struggling to escape. It knows how to work with cattle and can perform many ranch skills with little or no guidance from its rider. A cowboy can ride his Quarter Horse hard while rounding up cattle for branding and then leave it saddled and tied to a fence rail for hours waiting to be ridden again. For these reasons, Quarter Horses are by far the most popular horses used on cattle ranches today.

A good cow horse must be willing to wait until its work is needed.

A good cow horse is invaluable. It has "cow sense," the instinct to work with cattle and the knowledge of how to control them. When ranchers are working cattle—moving a herd or roping calves for branding—things often happen too fast for the rider to give commands to his or her mount. The horse must often make its own decisions about how to keep

Two good cow horses on the range. The horse
on the right is pulling back on the rope to help hold
the steer. The one on the left is standing quietly,
waiting for its rider, even though it is not tied up.

the cattle in line. For example, if it sees a steer bolt from the
herd, it needs to dash right after the steer, moving to the outside and turning it back into the herd.

A cow horse is a partner with its rider. When a calf is
roped, the horse must pull back on the rope to tighten the
loop around the calf, and it must keep the rope taut, even
after the rider has jumped off to work on the roped animal.

Cattle have to be moved for many reasons. If the rancher
owns several pastures, the cattle may need to be moved now

and then from one pasture to another to ensure that they do not overgraze one area, damaging the grass so that it cannot grow back quickly. In the late spring or early summer, a herd must be brought to branding corrals so that the calves can be branded. And in the fall, when the cattle are big enough to sell for beef, they are moved to a railroad or to a feedlot. While some ranchers nowadays use motorcycles to herd their cattle, most still prefer horses, which are far quieter and cause much less stress to the cattle.

The Westphal boys, Scott and Chris, herd in cattle.
The horses are from cutting-horse stock. The one
on the right is not a Quarter Horse. It has Paint colors—
patches of white and dark. A horse with this color
pattern cannot be registered as a Quarter Horse.

Horses are also used to herd other horses. A rancher with a big spread needs to have many horses to carry out the work, and he or she may also raise horses for sale. Like cattle, horses need to be moved from one pasture to another now and then to avoid overgrazing.

Quarter Horses are not always ridden while working; they are strong enough to pull wagons, too. In the wintertime, when grass is not growing and what grass there is may be covered by snow, range animals must be fed every day. Bales of hay are loaded onto a wagon or sleigh pulled by horses and are brought to the pasture where the hungry animals wait to be fed. While many ranchers use powerful draft horses to pull the feed wagon, others hitch up their Quarter Horses to do the work.

Quarter Horses help bring
winter feed to cattle.
The big horse in the middle
is half Quarter Horse and
half Percheron, a breed
of large workhorse.

Types of Quarter Horses Today

Quarter Horses are used in various types of competition based on the qualities of the breed. Quarter Horse racing is now very popular, and many animals are especially bred for use in races. "Cutting," a competition featuring the Quarter Horse's ability to work with cattle, is also growing rapidly. Cutting Quarter Horses come from different breeding than racehorses. Quarter Horses are also featured in their own horse shows, with competitions for the best-looking horses and the best-trained ones under saddle. After many years of breeding in search of horses that can win at these different competitions, the American Quarter Horse today is almost several different breeds under one name.

4

Quarter Horse Shows

A horse show can feature many different events, including barrel racing, pole bending, and jumping. Quarter Horse shows may have a dozen or more different sorts of competitions, but the pleasure riding and halter classes are always included and are the most popular.

Halter Classes

Halter classes are the "beauty contests" of horse shows. The animals are judged on their conformation, meaning the way their bodies are put together. The closer the horse is to the ideal Quarter Horse in looks, the better it will do in halter classes. Over the years, the standards of Quarter Horse beauty have changed somewhat. For example, the very large jaws of Steel Dust horses are no longer favored, although the

This handsome palomino stallion, Walks Far Jack, shows
the strength and beauty of the old-style Quarter Horse.

jaws should be strong and well-developed. Largely because
of the popularity of Quarter Horse racing, Thoroughbreds
have been bred to Quarter Horses more and more, and this
has changed some Quarter Horse traits. For example, the
withers (shoulders) of the horse should be slightly taller
than the rump. In the old days, the rump was higher than the
shoulders. Good withers, however, are important in a riding
horse, for the front of the saddle rests on the withers, which
help hold it in place. The modern Quarter Horse also has a
more arched neck than the old-style horse because of Thoroughbred breeding.

Tardy Truckle is a modern style Quarter Horse stallion.
Notice that his legs and neck are longer than those of
Walks Far Jack. COURTESY OF JOEL GLEASON

The head of a Quarter Horse should be relatively short
and wide, with a straight nose and "kindly eyes." The ears
should be quite small and pointed. A good halter horse has
lots of muscle in its legs, both on the inside and outside. Its
front legs are set well apart and are very straight. The lower
leg bones, called the cannon bones, are short in both front
and hind legs. A good Quarter Horse has a short back and a
deep chest. Altogether, it should have the appearance of great
strength and power.

Horses competing in a halter class.

In halter classes, the horses are shown wearing only a halter—a headpiece of leather straps much like a bridle but without a bit in the mouth. They are led around the ring by a handler. In addition to noting the animals' conformation, the judges watch how they move, looking for graceful and relaxed horses. A halter horse should also be well-behaved and respond to its handler's commands willingly.

Pleasure Classes

The Western Pleasure and English Pleasure classes at horse shows are always popular events. In Western Pleasure, the rider wears a western hat and cowboy boots, and rides a western saddle with a horn. The horses are asked to walk, trot, and lope (slow canter) in both directions around the ring. They are also stopped in the center of the ring, and each

A Western Pleasure competitor.

rider must make his or her horse back up on command.

In English Pleasure, an English saddle is used, and the rider wears a hard hat covered by black velvet as well as a riding coat. The horses walk, trot, and canter, and the rider must post (move up and down) in rhythm with the horse's trot. In all pleasure classes, the horses must be well trained and well behaved. These competitions are in a way the heart of a horse show, for they give owners of different ages and degrees of experience a chance to compete. There are pleasure classes for children of different ages and for owners and horses with different degrees of experience.

An English Pleasure competitor.

Becoming a Champion

The American Quarter Horse Association (AQHA), which keeps records for the breed and which sponsors shows, sets the standards for recognizing superior horses. Horses that are successful in racing or in horse shows can earn a "Register of Merit;" these horses may have the initials "ROM" after their names. To achieve the ROM, a racehorse must be able to run fast. The way the ROM is determined for race horses is complicated and is based on the speed of the horse and/or how well the horse does in races. For other Quarter Horses, the animal must win at least ten points at Quarter Horse shows in any event, not including halter classes. The points are awarded on the basis of the animal's place in the class and the number of horses entered.

It is much more difficult for a horse to become an AQHA Champion. In order to achieve this honor, a horse must win at least thirty-five points, in at least five different shows, with at least five different judges. A champion must show good Quarter Horse conformation, for at least fifteen of the points

Sheesa Tardy Bell was the Reserve Yearling for Montana in 1984. The points she earns may help her become a champion Quarter Horse.

This foal is a prizewinner.

must be in halter classes. It must also be well-trained, for at least fifteen of the points must be in performance classes, again with some of the points earned at large shows.

The ultimate honor for a Quarter Horse is to become an AQHA Supreme Champion. Very few horses achieve this recognition, for they must earn many points at top shows, including being named the Grand Champion of at least two big shows under different judges, and they must perform well on the race track. In addition, a Supreme Champion must earn performance points in calf roping, steer roping, or cutting, as well as in either riding or jumping classes. An AQHA Supreme Champion represents the ideal all around "using horse," which can perform a variety of tasks and which is beautiful as well.

5

The Quarter Horse in Action

The ability of the Quarter Horse to perform in action is tested on the ranch, in the show ring, and at rodeos. In local shows, family horses and working ranch horses often compete for honors as the fastest, most agile, or best trained animal. But in big shows and in rodeos, the contestants are professionals who stand to win big money.

Cow Horse Competition

The ultimate test of a cow horse is, of course, its ability to work cattle. One exciting way to test this talent is in calf roping. The roper takes along two lariats, sometimes called lassos, on his saddle. In addition, he has a "piggin' string," which is used to tie the calf's legs. He holds it between his

A contestant gets ready to rope a calf.

The rope finds its mark around the calf's neck.

The horse puts on its brakes, and the
rope tightens as the contestant dashes
to tie up the calf.

teeth or carries it tucked under his belt. The horse and rider
stand ready to go behind a ribbon barrier that is next to the
chute from which the calf comes running. Horse and rider
dash out after the calf. The horse must run at top speed and
position itself so that the rider can get a good shot at the calf
with the spinning lariat. If the first rope misses, the roper
tries again with the second. All the while his horse is dodging this way and that with the calf.

If the animal is successfully roped, the rider jumps off the
horse to tie the calf, while the horse must put on its brakes
instantly, pulling the loop taut around the calf's head. While

the roper works, the horse must stand alone, holding the calf steady. After the calf is tied, the cowboy returns to his horse. It takes a well-trained horse with an even temperament to perform well in roping. It must be able to charge full tilt from a standing start, run after the dodging calf, then stop suddenly and stand calmly without a rider to guide it. Since calf roping is judged on speed, any slowness or misstep by the horse can lose precious time in the event. Even in roping contests that are open to all breeds, the vast majority of the horses are Quarter Horses, because of their special combination of agility, speed, and even temperament.

Team roping involves two riders who cooperate in running down a steer. The "header" moves out and tosses a lariat over the steer's horns. Then the "heeler" ropes both hind legs with his rope. Team roping is a real challenge for the horses. The header's horse must dash out at top speed. The roper must snag the horns. Then the heading horse must position the steer for the heeler. The heeler's horse must know to back up as soon as the hind legs are caught. Both jobs require horses with speed, calm dispositions, and expert training.

In team roping, one contestant ropes the horns, then his partner ropes the hind legs.

Show and Rodeo Races

Horse shows and rodeos both feature the exciting barrel race. A Quarter Horse's agility and ability to attain speed quickly make it a favorite mount for this event. Three barrels are placed in a triangle. Horse and rider must run a cloverleaf pattern around the three barrels as quickly as possible. After rounding the third barrel, the pair must gallop back to the start/finish line at top speed. The winning pair is the one that completes the course in the shortest time without knocking over a barrel.

Barrel racing.

Pole bending. The horse and rider are heading for the last pole.
You can see the rest of the poles in the background.

Another test of speed and agility is pole bending, which is
popular in western horse shows.. Six poles are set twenty-one
feet apart. Horse and rider speed down to the farthest pole.
Then they must weave back between the poles, circling the
one closest to the starting line and weave their way again to
the farthest one. Then they dash back to the start/finish line.
Again, the fastest pair wins the race.

Trick Riding

Riding skill has always been valued in cattle country for ob-
vious reasons. Cowboys and Indians both liked to develop
their riding ability and show off their skills. Today, professional riders can make a living by mastering spectacular feats
of horsemanship. Because of its reliability and athletic ability, the Quarter Horse is often favored by trick riders.

Marvin Walchuck is a trick rider who trusts his life to his Quarter Horse. On the following two pages he is shown performing one of his tricks.

From the riding position shown on the preceding page he swings down one side of the horse, comes over its back, and lands facing backward on the horses neck. The horse must gallop evenly throughout the performance, despite the shifting weight of the rider.

6

Cutting Horses

The ability to work with cattle and other animals has been vital in the development of the American Quarter Horse. Even an old, slow Quarter Horse will perk up when ridden out into a pasture to herd cows. On a ranch, one of the most important tasks for horses to perform is to separate certain individuals from the herd, such as sick, crippled, or old animals. The term "cutting" refers to this process; one animal is "cut" from the herd. In ranch work, the group of cattle to which the animal is added after being removed from the herd is called the cut. The word cutting now applies to the sport in which horses compete to see which is the most able and agile in keeping a lone cow separated from the herd. The cow tries to get back to its companions while the horse prevents it from doing so.

Cutting has become increasingly popular in recent years and is now a well-known national sport. Any breed of horse

Chris Westphal uses his cutting horse to herd cattle.

can be used for cutting, but by far the most popular is the American Quarter Horse. The National Cutting Horse Association, which regulates cutting competitions, has over 12,000 members in all fifty states and several foreign countries, but 60 percent of cutting horses are in the state of Texas. With the increasing popularity of cutting, however, some cutting horses now even come from eastern states and have never seen a ranch. Their owners and riders are often doctors, lawyers, and other professional people who love horses but live in cities.

Only race horses are worth more and earn more money for their owners than do cutting horses. The best cutting stallions are worth millions of dollars each, and top mares may sell for over $100,000. Breeding fees for stallions can be over $10,000. Prizes in cutting events can run into thousands of dollars. At the World Championship Cutting Horse Futurity, held in Forth Worth, Texas, early in December, three-year-old horses that have never been shown before compete for a top prize of over $250,000, with the total prize money over a million-and-a-half dollars. Cutting has definitely become "big business." Even so, many of the competitors in cutting are western ranchers whose children grow up on horseback and who use their less valuable cutting horses in their pastures to work their cattle.

Cutting Competition

Cutting competitions are held in indoor or outdoor arenas with dirt or sand surfaces. A small herd of cattle is kept at one end of the arena by two riders called "herd holders." Two other riders, called "turn-back men," are also in the arena. The competing horses and riders take turns working the cattle in the order they are drawn by the judge. Each 2 ½ minute turn is called a "go-round." During this time, the horse demonstrates its ability to work a cow. At the start of a go-round, the competing horse and rider walk slowly toward

Buddy Westphal, riding his horse Nu Way To Go, moves quietly into the herd.

the cattle. Very quietly, they enter the herd and maneuver a small group of cattle away from the rest, looking for a cow that can be easily separated from its companions. While in the herd and making the cut, the rider can use the reins gently to tell the horse which cow to cut out. This "herd work" must be done as calmly as possible so that the animals are not disturbed. As a cow is selected, it is gently persuaded to move away from the herd, out into the open part of the arena.

When the cow discovers it is all alone, the fun begins. The cow is standing in the middle of the arena facing a mounted cutting horse, and it does its best maneuvering to get past the horse and return to the herd. At this point, the horse is on its own, using instinct and athletic ability to control the cow. The reins swing loose, and the rider concentrates on staying aboard his or her twisting, turning mount. The horse stands with lowered head, eyes riveted on the cow, as if reading its

Deep in the herd, Buddy looks for a promising cow.

A good cutting horse stares right into the cow's eyes as it works.

As the cow tries to escape, the horse ducks and dives to keep the cow in its place.

mind. When the cow swings to one side, the horse swings with it. A lunge to the other side brings a counter lunge by the horse. It is like a dance, except that one partner is unwilling.

A good cutting horse crouches low on its hind legs, swinging its front feet back and forth with the cow. The sudden movements of the trapped animal require equally rapid responses from the horse. A cutting horse is an ultimate animal athlete that must be lightning quick and agile, with flexible, strong joints that can take great stress. Cutting horses often wear protective boots to protect them from injuries caused by kicking or stepping on themselves as they swing back and forth, frequently crossing their legs to keep their balance. The horse has to think for itself, outguessing the cow while the rider sits passively on its back, holding onto the saddle horn with one hand to stay aboard.

Cutting horses can get down low on their hind legs.

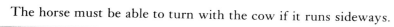

The horse must be able to turn with the cow if it runs sideways.

At the fence, the horse must turn back
toward the center with the cow.

When the cow runs to one side in an attempt to get past its opponent, the horse must turn with it and run a parallel course, matching the cow stride for stride. At the side of the arena, the horse must get the cow to turn and run back the other way across the arena and not let it dash along the wall back to the herd. This is a very tricky part of cutting, for the horse must be just a step ahead of the cow to control it. At all times, the horse must keep itself between the cow and the herd.

Before long, most cows give up and realize they won't be able to get past the nimble horse that keeps outmaneuvering them. When the cow stands still or turns away from the horse, the contestant can quit working it and go into the herd again to repeat the whole process. In one 2½ minute go-round, the horse should work two or three cows.

A herd holder watches the cutting team work.

With his back to the camera, a turn-back man
goes after an escaping cow.

During the go-round, the herd holders keep the cattle from straying. The turn-back men help startle a cow into facing the cutting team, and they keep it from running away into the far part of the arena. The herd holders and turn-back men are usually other contestants in the competition who are chosen by the cutter; the contestants take turns helping one another in this way.

Judging the Go-Round

Contestants are given a score ranging from 60 to 80 points. Good scores are usually in the low 70s. There are many ways to lose points. Not entering the herd deeply at least once while choosing a cow and scattering the cattle are examples. Any signals given by the rider to the horse through the reins while the horse is working the cow also results in loss of points, as does allowing the cow to get back into the herd while being worked. Credit is given for doing things right, too. For example, entering the herd quietly without disturbing the cattle and driving the cow far enough from the herd before working it will add points to the score. The western look is preserved at cutting contests by requiring the rider to wear western clothes—a western hat, cowboy boots, and a western style shirt.

The horse and rider are as one as they quietly enter the herd, separating out an animal gently and moving it unknowingly to the center of the arena. Then suddenly, the mood changes, from peace and quiet to explosive action as the cow and horse dance back and forth, matching their wits and bodies in a fast-moving drama of beauty and excitement.

Cutting Horse Qualities

Cutting horses are judged completely on their ability to work cattle. Their looks do not matter at all, nor does their breeding. A cutting horse does not even have to be any particular breed, as long as it can cut cattle. Because they need to be agile and quick, cutting horses tend to be smaller than other show horses and race horses. While they are strong and well-muscled, they also lack the very pronounced heavy muscles of many halter horses. A cutting horse must have strong legs, for the twisting and turning involved in cutting put great strain on the legs. Its hind legs are not always

While Doc Sox is a handsome cutting horse, he is not as big-boned as most halter horses.

straight, and they are often more angled than those of a halter horse. The front legs of some very successful cutting horses are a bit crooked. Rarely is a cutting horse also successful as a halter horse.

Much of the ability to work cattle is bred into the cutting horse. It somehow knows how to face off a cow and how to keep it under control. There is an important balance in the horse's aggressive moves towards the cow. It must dominate the animal but not actually attack it. Some cutting horses are too aggressive and try to bite or strike a cow with a hoof. This sort of behavior must be stopped immediately, for it is not acceptable in competition.

John Nash, M.D., cuts with his horse,
Doc Simple Simon, a son of Doc Bar.

Even though cutting ability comes naturally, these horses need careful training to bring out their best. They need to learn to go into the herd quietly and to respond to the slightest movements of the reins while there. Most cutting horses need to learn how to move their front legs while working the cow. They must learn to run parallel to the cow when it heads for a side of the arena and to wheel with it, without going past, while turning it back to the center. The natural aggression of the horse towards the cow makes is especially hard for it to learn to run next to the cow rather than towards it. Training a fine cutting horse can take two years before its first competition and, when done by a professional trainer, can cost $1,000 a month.

Not all Quarter Horses are good cutting horses. As with other talents, cutting ability "runs in the family." For this reason, many of the best cutting horses have similar names, indicating similar ancestry. Doc Bar, for example, is a recent top stallion. While he never cut himself, his offspring have been especially talented. Many of the best cutting horses today have "Doc" or "Bar" in their names, indicating that they are descended from this special horse.

7
Quarter Horse Racing

While Quarter Horse racing was revived only in the 1940s, it has become very popular at some American racetracks. Tracks may alternate periods of Thoroughbred races with those for Quarter Horses or offer races for both breeds on the same days. While Thoroughbred races are often run at distances of over a mile, most Quarter Horse races are no longer

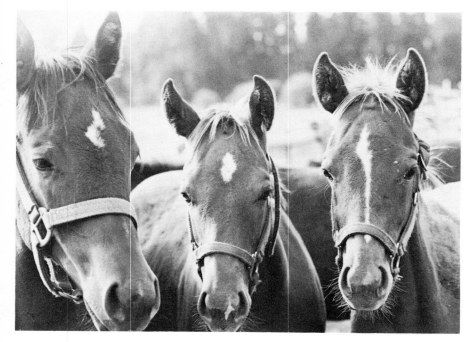

These young Quarter Horses will grow up to be racers.

than a quarter of a mile. The shortest race is only 220 yards. With such short distances, an explosive start and blinding early speed are required for success.

Before the Race

Horses must be carefully trained and prepared for racing. Their bodies must be in top condition to perform well. Race horses have their workouts during the morning, when they are taken to a track and exercised in different ways, depending on the stage of training. Sometimes they jog slowly around the track several times. Other times they run short spurts of speed. Trainers need to know their horses well to prepare them so that they are in top condition the day of a race. Thoroughbreds need to learn strategy for races, such as how to wait for an opening to overtake other horses and how to go around turns. Quarter Horses are just trained to run as fast as they can, straight ahead. Only one distance for Quarter Horse races, 870 yards, requires them to go around a turn.

A racing Quarter Horse gets its morning workout at Bay Meadows. PHOTO BY DOROTHY HINSHAW PATENT

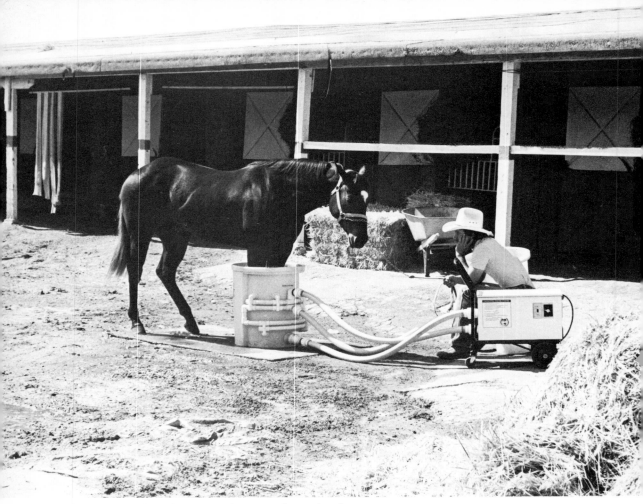

A whirlpool bath is sometimes used to stimulate
blood circulation to the front legs of racehorses.
PHOTO BY DOROTHY HINSHAW PATENT

Before being allowed to race, a Quarter Horse must qual-
ify by running before a track official called a racing secretary.
It must break properly from the starting gate and run while
the secretary times the run, watching the horse to make sure
it is in sound condition. This protects both the horse and the
betting public.

Often, Quarter Horses are worked very little during the
last days before a race. They are kept hungry for running,

Before and after a race,
the jockeys are weighed,
along with the saddle,
to make sure the horses
carry the correct weight.

eager to go, so that they are mentally as well as physically prepared for those all important split seconds of the race.

On the big day, many horses seem to know that a race is in the air. Some become so excited that they must be closed up in a dark stall with no view of the outside world in order to keep them from using up all their energy pacing about. A familiar person spends the day with the racer to help keep it from becoming too nervous.

About twenty minutes before a race is to start, the horses are led into the paddock area to be saddled. In the paddock, there are partitioned areas for saddling and an arena where the horses can be led around to help calm them, and for the public to view them. When they are ready, the horses are mounted by the jockeys and are led to the track. Riders on horses called lead ponies help bring the horses out. On the track, the racers are warmed up. It is very important at this time to get their muscles loosened and warm. Quarter Horse races are so short that the animals must put all their effort out from the start. If their muscles are not prepared for the great strain, they could be hurt during the race.

After being saddled, the horses at Sunland Park in New Mexico are brought out to be mounted where bettors can look them over.

The horses are led onto
the track by lead ponies.

They're Off!

Just before the race begins, the horses are led into the starting
gate. The starting gate has separate metal stalls for the horses
where they wait for the starting bell. The start is the most
important part of a Quarter Horse race. It is almost impossi-
ble in only a quarter mile to make up for a slow start. The
horses must be bursting at the seams to run and be ready to
explode from the gate. For this reason, Quarter Horses are
given plenty of training in making the fastest possible start.
Some horses are so excited in the starting gate that they try
to run forward as the gate is closed in front of them. Since

they cannot go forward, they fall over backward, endangering themselves and their jockeys. Such a horse must be restrained. A special "flipping halter" which is anchored to the stall is clipped to the nervous horse's bridle so that it cannot hurt itself before the race begins. The flipping halter releases when the starting gate opens.

When the starting bell goes off, the doors to all the stalls spring open at the same time, and the horses leap forward. A Quarter Horse race is run straight in one direction, with no turns (except in the 870-yard race), and is over in less than twenty-three seconds. By the second stride, the horses are running at top speed—up to 45 miles per hour. Luck as well as speed can play a role in determining the winner. If two horses bump into one another, chances are slim that they can recover in time in such a short race.

As the horses plunge over the finish line, a special camera takes their picture. Because they are so short, Quarter Horse races may be close, and photos are often needed to determine the winner.

Within seconds, the race is over and the winner crosses the finish line (at striped post).

After the race, the horses must be slowed down again.

The World's Richest Quarter Horse Race

The race with the biggest money to the winners is the All American Futurity, run on Labor Day at Ruidoso Downs, New Mexico. The winner gets a million dollars, which means it earns over $45,000 per second during the race. Another million and a half or more is split among the other nine entrants. The decision as to which horses run in this race

The winner goes to the winner's circle for a photo.
On the left, you can see a jockey going to be weighed.

takes a long time. Breeders nominate their most promising foals by putting up $50 per horse twenty months before the race. During those months, seven more payments must be made, each bigger than the previous one, to keep the horse in the running. In 1984, 2,600 horses were originally nominated, but with each payment, more and more were dropped from the list. By the end, owners have to put up $3,100 to allow a horse to try out for the race. If an owner has a promising horse that was not nominated as a foal, he can still get in on the fun for a more substantial fee.

The final entrants in the big race are chosen in two preparatory races, which narrows the field down to the final ten horses. Even the tenth placing horse in the Futurity wins money—over $50,000. Consolation races are held, too, for horses that did not make the final ten, with the result that thirty other horses split another half million dollars among them.

Eastex wins the 1984 All American Futurity at Ruidoso Downs and takes home a million dollars. The total purse for the race that year was $2,530,000. COURTESY OF RUIDOSO-SUNLAND, INC.

Breeding Racing Quarter Horses

Quarter Horse racing is big business, and breeders work hard to produce the best racers they can. A good racehorse has certain physical characteristics. Its shoulder is angled so that its front legs can reach far out while running. Its hip bones must be long so that it can stretch its hind legs way under its body to produce a long stride. Its back should be short and strong, and its neck long. Thoroughbreds have all these traits, while Quarter Horses often do not, even though they can take off fast from a standing start. For this reason, and to introduce more stamina, breeders often mate Thoroughbreds to their racing Quarter Horses. As a result, most racing Quarter Horses are over 50 percent Thoroughbred.

Not all Thoroughbreds mix well with Quarter Horses, and

Here you can see the angled shoulder
and long hip that make a fast racehorse.

Thoroughbred and Quarter Horse mares graze together in the pasture.

the animals used are chosen with care. Those that do improve the racing ability of the Quarter Horse, however, can have enormous influence. Three Bars, a Thoroughbred stallion that died in 1968, for example, produced many successful racing Quarter Horses and is considered the "granddad" of racing Quarter Horse sires.

A Quarter Horse that is as much as 15/16ths Thoroughbred is given "appendixed" (tentative) Quarter Horse registration and can run on the track with those papers. A Quarter Horse identifier measures the horse and examines its pedigree to determine if it meets all the standards for the breed. If it does, it can be registered as a genuine Quarter Horse. When a pasture is full of Thoroughbreds and racing Quarter Horses, however, it can sometimes be difficult to tell the two breeds apart.

8

Your Own Quarter Horse

Not only is a Quarter Horse an especially good family horse, but a trained Quarter Horse or part Quarter Horse can usually be bought for a reasonable amount of money. Just how much depends on the part of the country and the market for horses at the time. But if you want a horse that is registered as belonging to a particular breed, your best buy may be an American Quarter Horse.

Choosing Your Horse

Buying a horse can be tricky. It is easy to fall in love with the first animal you go to look at. But it is very important to get a mount that will be reliable and good natured. The most friendly, lovable horse in the world is not much use unless it

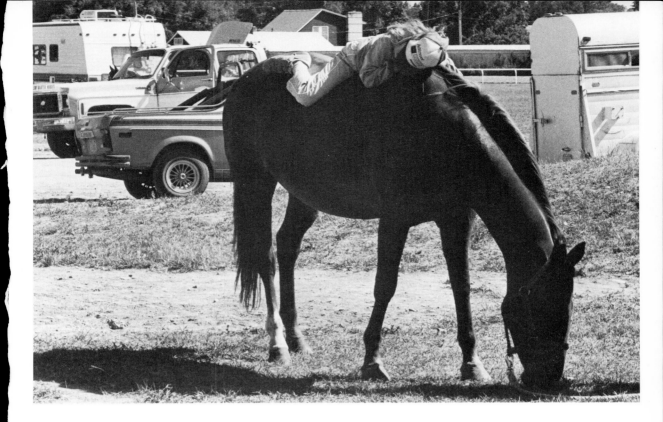

can be safely and comfortably ridden. The least expensive, most dependable horse is likely to be a gelding (a male horse that has been castrated) about ten years old that has been a treasured family horse. Geldings have more even temperaments than mares, and stallions (males that can breed) are usually too difficult for children and inexperienced adults to handle. A ten-year-old horse is old enough to be well trained, and calm but young enough to give many years of companionship and riding enjoyment.

Before you buy a horse, you should check with people you know who have horses for advice about making your choice. You might also contact the local chapter of the American Quarter Horse Association to find out more about buying this breed. Try to get someone who knows horses to go with

you to look over the available animals. Ride each horse at all the gaits to make sure it is well behaved and comfortable to be aboard. Remember that a choppy walk can become very unpleasant after an hour or even less. Before making a final decision, have the horse examined by a veterinarian.

Choose your horse according to your riding ability and the ways you want to use it. If you want a family horse for trail riding, you will want to pick a quiet, gentle horse. But if you are interested in competing in particular events, you should try to get a horse with the appropriate breeding and training. You will need a fast horse for barrel racing, for example, and a well-trained one for pleasure classes.

The annual National Bison Range trail ride attracts many horses and riders each year.

Activities for Kids with Horses.

Whatever kind of horse you own, even if it is not registered, there are many group activities available. There are special clinics which can teach you about riding and caring for your horse. There are riding clubs and 4-H Clubs which sponsor trail rides and shows. In many areas, troups of young riders work together to carry out group maneuvers with their horses and perform at horse shows and fairs. High schools in almost half the states all over the country are participating in the National High School Rodeo competitions.

If you own a registered American Quarter Horse, you can join the American Junior Quarter Horse Association for only a few dollars a year and compete in Youth Shows sponsored by the AQHA. These shows feature eighteen different events, including halter, barrel racing, roping, riding, and

Western Riding competition in horse shows tests both horse and rider.

pleasure categories. The shows give you an opportunity to work with your horse and train together for whatever types of competiton you choose to enter. Both you and your horse can benefit from the learning and challenge associated with participating in shows. You can also meet other children with horses and make new friends.

By entering Youth Shows, you can earn points towards special awards reserved for young people—Showmanship at Halter, All-Around Performance Trophy, and Youth AQHA Champion. But even if you are not interested in competing with your horse, owning, riding, and caring for your own animal can be a very special part of your life.

Places to Write for More Information

American Junior Quarter Horse Association
Amarillo, TX 79168

American Quarter Horse Association
Amarillo, TX 79168

National Cutting Horse Association
P.O. Box 12155
Fort Worth, TX 76121

National High School Rodeo Association
Kenneth Ivester, Ex. Sec./Treas.
118 North Third St.
Douglas, WY 82633

Publications of Interest

Cuttin' Hoss Chatter
National Cutting Horse Assn.
P.O. Box 12155
Fort Worth, TX 76121

Eastern/Western Quarter Horse Journal
Drawer 690
Middleboro, MA 02346

The Quarter Horse Journal
American Quarter Horse Assn.
P.O. Box 9105
Amarillo, TX 79105

Quarter Horse News
P.O. Box 9707
Ft. Worth, TX 76107

Quarter Horse Track
Track Publishers, Inc.
P.O. Box 9648
Fort Worth, TX 76107

Quarter Racing Record
P.O. Box 2473
Fort Worth, TX 76113

Speedhorse
P.O. Box 1000
Norman, OK 73070

The American Quarter Horse Association has many films about Quarter Horses available for use, free of charge. Some films are informational, others include instruction in such areas as basic training of horses and judging Quarter Horse competitions. Films need to be reserved in advance. Some films are also available for purchase on video tapes. For more information, phone 806-376-4811, or write: AQHA Films
American Quarter Horse Association
Amarillo, TX 79168

Glossary

appendixed Quarter Horse registration: An appendixed horse is one which will be officially registered as a Quarter Horse only after it wins a certain number of competitions and is examined for Quarter Horse conformation.

barrel race: A timed race in which the horse and rider run a cloverleaf course around three barrels.

bloodlines: The hereditary background of a horse; its parents and other ancestors.

calf roping: A timed contest in which the rider ropes a calf, dismounts, and ties the calf's legs.

canter: The gait of a horse between a trot and a gallop. One front foot and the opposite hind foot hit the ground at the same time.

conformation: The physical appearance of an animal.

cow horse: A horse used to herd and control cattle.

cutting horse: A horse used in competition testing its ability to separate a cow from a herd and keep it from returning to the herd.

dam: The mother of an animal.

distance horse: A horse that can run fast for long distances.

flipping halter: A special halter used in Quarter Horse racing to keep a nervous horse from trying to run before the starting gate is opened.

foal: A baby horse.

gait: A manner of walking or running. A horse's natural gaits are the walk, trot, canter, and gallop.

gallop: The fastest gait of a horse. Each foot hits the ground separately, and all four feet are off the ground simultaneously part of the time.

gelding: A male horse that has been castrated. Geldings are calmer than stallions.

go-round: A single timed test of a cutting horse's ability.

halter: A headpiece for a horse to which a lead rope can be attached.

halter class: A competition in which horses are judged on their conformation. The only thing a horse wears at this time is a halter.

hand: A measure of a horse's height. A hand is four inches. The height is taken by measuring the number of hands from the ground to the top of the withers.

heat: In racing, a "race" sometimes consists of several individual races. Each of these races is called a heat.

herd holder: A helper in cutting-horse competition who helps keep the cows together at one end of the arena.

jockey: The rider in a horse race.

lariat: A lasso.

lasso: A long rope with a sliding noose at one end, used to catch cattle or other animals.

lope: A slow canter.

mare: A female horse.

mustang: A western name for a wild horse.

paddock: The area where race horses are saddled before a race.

pleasure class: A competition in which a horse shows its training for riding. The horse must obey the rider's commands when asked to change gaits, stop, back up, etc.

pole bending: A timed race in which horse and rider must wind through a series of poles as fast as possible.

rodeo: A show featuring a number of events, mostly for horses and riders, such as calf roping, bronc riding, bull riding, etc.

short horse: A horse good at racing a short distance.

short horse racing: Races held over a distance of a quarter mile or less.

sire: The male parent of a horse.

sprinter: A horse that runs its fastest right from the beginning of a race.

stallion: A male horse that still has its sex organs and can therefore be used for breeding.

steers: Male cattle that have been castrated.

team roping: A competition in which two riders chase and rope a steer.

trot: The second gait of a horse in which the legs move as in a walk but faster.

turn-back men: Helpers at a cutting competition who keep the cow being worked from running away from the cutting horse and rider.

wean: To take an animal off its mother's milk.

winner's circle: The place to which the winning horse is led after a race, where its picture is taken along with the owners, trainer, and jockey.

withers: The top of the shoulder of a horse.

Index

DATE DUE

OCT 3 1994		
NOV - 3 1994		
JAN 1 0 1995		
FEB 8 1995		
APR - 5 1995		
5/2/95		
66.92 JAN 26 99		
JAN 26 99		
MAY 03 '99		
DEC 06 '04		